Preface

This small book is the perfect companion to a tour of The Black Watch Museum and we hope that it will add to the experience of exploring the regiment's history as it is portrayed in the wide-ranging exhibits in Balhousie Castle. In the pages that follow will be found not only a brief history of the regiment from its earliest days in the 18th century but also reproductions of just a few of the many treasures that help us to tell the story of Scotland's best known regiment.

The Museum does indeed tell the story of The Black Watch but it also tells the story of Britain through more than 250 years of its imperial and post-imperial history. It would be stretching a point to suggest that The Black Watch was present at every single significant military action since its formation in 1739 but it would not be too far from the truth to do so. We are very proud of the contribution that Black Watch men have made to that history, not because every battle was won (there were many that were not) but because of the manner in which we have made that contribution. No doubt there have been one or two lapses over the years but the overwhelming experience of Black Watch soldiering has been characterized by professional skill, gallantry, humanity, fortitude in the face of adversity, great style and pride in appearance, a splendid sense of humour and above all by an unsurpassed esprit de corps. These qualities have attracted to us over the years many admirers amongst friend and foe alike. That is why we take so much pride in opening our doors to the general public so that they can share with us that sense of pride and admiration for what Black Watch men have achieved whenever, even today in 2011, the name and the regiment's famous red hackle have been seen doing the nation's business.

We hope that this book will encourage you to visit the Museum if you have not already done so. If you have bought this book after touring the exhibits we hope that it will serve as a memento of your time at Balhousie Castle. Thank you for coming to see us and please come again. You will be more than welcome.

Lieutenant General Sir Alistair Irwin KCB CBE
Chairman of The Black Watch Museum Trust

The Black Watch
(Royal Highland Regiment)

A short history of the Regiment in peace and war

The Black Watch Castle & Museum

Published by Perth and Kinross Heritage Trust 2011
All images and text are copyright
© The Black Watch Museum Trust 2011

Printed and Bound by Farquhar and Son Ltd., Perth

ISBN 978-0-9564427-4-1

The Black Watch
CASTLE & MUSEUM

PERTH AND KINROSS
HERITAGE TRUST

Cover illustration: The 2nd Battalion at Glasgow Green, 1758.

A Private of the 43rd (Highland) Regiment, 1742, from a sketch in Illustrations of the Cloathing of the British Army, a volume prepared by order of George II.

1. Introduction

Over the centuries, The Black Watch has instilled the traditions and attitudes of this legendary Regiment on generations of Black Watch men. The Black Watch is known across the world as one of the most famous fighting units. Mere mention of the name is enough to conjure up visions of bravery, valour, true Scottish grit and determination. It is perhaps not surprising, since there can hardly be a corner of the globe in which The Black Watch has not served with distinction.

The Black Watch traces its origins to six Independent Companies raised in 1725, on the recommendation of General Wade, then Commander-in-Chief in Scotland. Three of the Companies were commanded by Campbells, and the other three by a Fraser, a Grant and a Munro. The Companies varied in size: the larger consisted of 100 men and the smaller of 70. The principal function was to keep the peace in the Highlands. They were "The Watch on the Braes". These Companies, with the later addition of another four Companies, were regimented, in 1739, under the command of the Earl of Crawford, who was appointed Colonel. They were first known as Crawford's Highlanders. The Regiment first mustered at Aberfeldy in May 1740.

Titles

While the Regiment was initially numbered the 43rd, it became the 42nd in 1751, a title it was to make famous over the centuries. In 1758 the Regiment was granted the title 'Royal' by the King in recognition of the Regiment's service. At this time it known as the 42nd (The Royal Highland) Regiment of Foot. In 1882 it became known as the 1st and 2nd Battalions The Black Watch (Royal Highlanders) and in 1934 it became The Black Watch (Royal Highland Regiment).

Am Freichan Dubh

In Gaelic, they were known as *Am Freichan Dubh,* or The Black Watch, because of the dark tartan they wore, and because their function was to police or 'watch' the Highlands. The original uniform was a twelve yard long plaid of the dark tartan which is now so well known as The Black Watch tartan.

Broadsword, dated to 1725.

Objects from the Museum collection relating to the Early Years of the Regiment (from top left to bottom right): glass bottle dated to 1742; powder horn used in the North American campaigns; broadsword dated to 1725; officer's dirk; pistol dated to circa 1745; powder horn used in the North American campaigns.

2. Early Years

The Mutiny (1743)

Many of the recruits spoke only Gaelic and understood that their engagement was for service in Scotland only. In 1743, the Regiment was ordered to London to be reviewed by the King. During the march through England, rumours began to spread that the unit was to be sent to the West Indies. At that time, this was virtually a death sentence because of climatic conditions and disease.

When they arrived in London, the King had embarked for Hanover and they were reviewed by Marshal Wade instead. Rumours regarding the West Indies continued. So much so, that over 100 of the men mutinied. They reached as far as Northampton, where they were persuaded to surrender. Three of the leaders, Farquhar Shaw and the cousins Malcolm and Samuel MacPherson, were shot in the Tower of London. The remainder were split into small groups and sent to various other units. Meanwhile the main body of the Regiment had been sent to Flanders.

Farquhar Shaw.

Fontenoy (1745)

The first major campaign in which the Regiment took part was the War of the Austrian Succession. In 1745 Lord John Murray, son of the Duke of Atholl, was appointed Colonel of the Regiment. The 'blooding' of the Regiment took place at the Battle of Fontenoy, 11th May 1745. Although a defeat for the British Forces, the conduct of the Highlanders under Lieutenant Colonel Sir Robert Munro of Fowlis was noted. They were referred to as the 'Highland Furies'.

The Black Watch at Fontenoy, 11th May 1745 by W. Skeoch Cumming.

The '45

In October 1745, 11 regiments, including Murray's Highlanders, were ordered to return to Britain. Murray's Regiment was kept at Deal, in Kent, throughout the 1745 Jacobite Uprising. Three additional Companies had been raised, one of which was taken prisoner by the Jacobites at the Battle of Prestonpans. Although regiments were known by the name of their Colonels, there was an order of precedence in which The Black Watch were 43rd. With the disbandment of Oglethorpe's Regiment in 1749, it became the 42nd. Two years later, by the Royal Warrant of 1st July 1751, regiments became known by their numbers. This led to the Regiment being referred to as 'The Gallant Forty-Twa'.

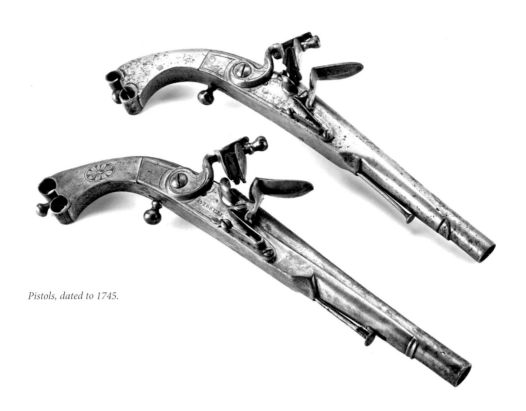

Pistols, dated to 1745.

The 2nd Battalion at Glasgow Green, 1758.

North America (1756-67 and 1776-89)

During the eighteenth-century, The Black Watch served twice in North America. The first was during the French Indian Wars of 1756-67. The best-known action was the Battle of Ticonderoga, 7th July 1758. Some 200 miles north of New York, Fort Ticonderoga was strategically important as a portage on the river between Canada and the British colonies. Occupied by the French under the name Fort Carillon, it was situated on a spit of land between Lake George and Lake Champlain. The defences consisted of entrenchments and a tall rampart. Large trees had been felled and were positioned in front of the rampart, with sharpened branches pointing outwards. After the initial attack failed, the 42nd, which had been in reserve, came forward impatiently. The Highlanders charged into felled trees, lopping off the sharpened branches with their broadswords. Some reached the ramparts, but were repulsed. The attack continued relentlessly but was a gallant failure. The loss to the regiment was 25 officers and 622 men killed and wounded. The fort eventually fell the following year.

The second period of service was during the Revolutionary Wars of 1776-89. On both occasions, at the end of their service soldiers were offered Land Grants to settle in North America. There was a settlement of men of The Black Watch from the latter campaign in the Nashwaak Valley in New Brunswick and some of their descendants still live there today.

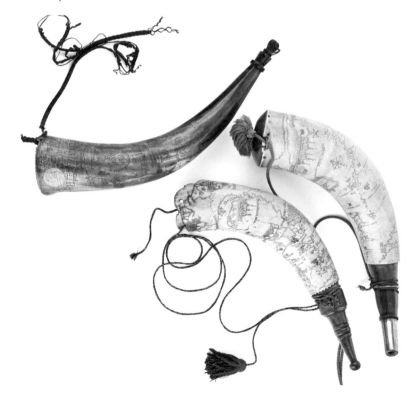

Carved powder horns, dated to the North American campaigns. The horns are illustrated with maps of North America, images of battle scenes and masonic symbols.

Broadsword, dated to the Battle of Fort Ticonderoga in 1758.

The Red Hackle

While the origin of the wearing of the Red Hackle is uncertain, there is evidence that it was worn by the 42nd in North America in the 1770s. Colonel Maitland commanded the 71st (Fraser's Highlanders) Regiment during the American War of Independence. After Maitland's death, his regiment was disbanded and officers and soldiers of the 71st joined The Black Watch, reputedly bringing the wearing of the Red Hackle to their new regiment.

A nineteenth-century tradition ascribes the award of the Red Hackle to an action at the battle of Geldermalsen in 1795. The 11th Light Dragoons retreated, leaving two field guns for the French. The Black Watch promptly mounted an attack and recovered the guns for which the Red Hackle was allegedly awarded. On the King's birthday on 4th June 1795, there was a parade at Royston in Hertfordshire, when a Red Hackle was given to every man on parade.

The red hackle.

It was not until 1822 that the Adjutant General issued an order, confirming that only The Black Watch would have the privilege of wearing the red "vulture feather" in their bonnets.

Alexandria (1801)

The French invasion of Egypt was primarily aimed at threatening Britain's access to India, and obtaining an overseas empire for France. The British army was under the command of Sir Ralph Abercrombie and on 21st March 1801 they fought off a night assault by several French columns. During the assault The Black Watch captured a French standard and Abercrombie was injured with a musket ball. It could not be extracted and he died seven days later. The French forces were eventually defeated and the British advanced upon Alexandria and laid siege to it. The French garrison surrendered on 2nd September 1801. Following the performance of the Regiment at the Battle of Alexandria, it was awarded the honour of bearing a Sphinx on the Colours and Regimental badges.

The Highland Society

The Highland Society presented a medal, designed by Sir Benjamin West, to various members of The Black Watch for the successful capture of a French standard at the Battle of Alexandria. Sixteen years later, on 18th June 1817, the Highland Society also presented the Regiment, then stationed at Armagh, with a magnificent silver vase for their gallantry.

The Highland Society vase.

3. The Napoleonic Wars and the Crimean War (1803-1855)

The Napoleonic War (1803-15)

The Napoleonic Wars were fought against Napoleon Bonaparte's France and a continually changing set of European alliances. Britain declared war on France on 18th May 1803 following the breakdown of the Treaty of Amiens. The Wars ended on 18th June 1815 with the defeat of Napoleon at Waterloo by The Duke of Wellington in command of an allied army.

The Peninsular War was fought from 1808 to 1814. This saw the Duke of Wellington emerge as the greatest allied military leader. The war began when the French invaded Portugal. France then turned on their ally Spain with the idea of controlling the entire Iberian Peninsula. The war saw a Spanish, Portuguese, British alliance slowly drive the French out of the Peninsula. The subsequent invasion of France led to Napoleon's abdication and exile.

The Battle Honours won during this period were: Corunna, Buscao, Fuentes D'Onor , Ciudad Rodrigo, Salamanca, Pyrenees, Nivelle, Nive, Orthez, Toulouse and Peninsula.

Military General Service Medal with Bars: Egypt and Talavera. The medal was issued in 1848, and only to survivors.

Waterloo and the Battle of Quatre Bras

Two days before the Battle of Waterloo, Napoleon's Deputy, Marshal Ney, launched a surprise attack on the cross roads of Quatre Bras. This was an attempt to cut off Wellington's armies from his Prussian allies. It was here that The Black Watch stood with other Regiments to face a numerically superior French force. Despite sustaining heavy casualties, they beat off both infantry and cavalry charges and held firm until reinforcements arrived to drive off the French attack. The stand of The Black Watch has gone down in history as one of the most heroic actions of the Napoleonic Wars. However, the events of that day have always been overshadowed by the final defeat of Napoleon at Waterloo two days later. Victory at Quatre Bras allowed Wellington to force Napoleon to meet him at Waterloo, his preferred choice of battleground. It also ensured that Prussian forces were able to reach Waterloo without any delay, which ultimately swung the battle in Wellington's favour. Without the actions of the brave men at Quatre Bras the final defeat of the French Emperor might never have happened.

Waterloo Medal.

The Black Watch at Bay by W.B. Wollen. The painting depicts the famous Battle of Quatre Bras, 16th June 1815.

Forward 42nd The Battle of the Alma. Lieutenant Peter Halkett of Pitfirrane is pictured in the painting carrying the Sovereign's Colour. He is buried in Dunfermline Abbey.

The Crimean War (1854-55)

The Crimean War was fought between the Russian Empire and an alliance of France, Great Britain, the Kingdom of Sardinia and the Ottoman Empire. The war was one part of a long-standing dispute between the major powers in Europe for control over the declining Ottoman Empire. The majority of the conflict took place on the Crimean Peninsula, with additional actions taking place in the Baltic Sea region and Turkey. The Black Watch was sent to the Crimea as part of the Highland Brigade along with 79th Cameron Highlanders and 93rd Highlanders. The Brigade was commanded by General Sir Colin Campbell. The Black Watch were involved in at the Battle of the Alma, the Battle of Balaklava and the Siege of Sebastopol. The Battle of the Alma, 20th September 1854, is usually considered the first battle of the Crimean War and took place in the vicinity of the River Alma in the Crimea. An Anglo-French force defeated the Russian army, which lost around 6,000 troops.

Crimean War medal, with Bars: Sebastopol, Inkerman, Balaklava and Alma.

Objects from the Museum
collections relating to the Crimean
War period (clockwise from
top left): wooden water bottle
of J. Duncan, feather bonnet
of Lieutenant Peter Halkett;
epaulettes of Halkett; officer's sash
of Halkett; pistol; Russian triptych,
gifted to members of the Regiment
after the Battle of the Alma in
recognition of their compassion;
tartan sash of Halkett.

Piper Muir, Privates Glen and Mackenzie and Colour Sergeant Gardner, photographed in 1856 upon return from the Crimea.

Major General Sir Robert Henry Dick of Tulliemet (1786-1846)

Dick was a soldier of distinction with a long-standing connection with The Black Watch. It was during his service with the Regiment that he took part in the Battle of Quatre Bras. During the Battle the Commanding Officer was killed and, as second in command, Dick assumed command. However, this was only for a few minutes, as he was soon wounded in the hip and shoulder, and he was unable to take any further part in the campaign. He was promoted to Lieutenant Colonel and command of the 42nd from June 1815 until 1828. Retiring from active service for ten years, he applied for re-employment in 1838. His distinguished career and long-standing connection with The Black Watch made him a most suitable Colonel for the 73rd Regiment. He died in 1846 at the Battle of Sobraon in India, from one of the last shots fired during the encounter.

Jacket and ceremonial sword belonging to Major General Dick.

4. The 73rd Regiment

The 73rd Regiment plays an important part in the early history of the Black Watch. It was first raised as a 2nd Battalion of the 42nd (The Royal Highland) Regiment in 1779 but became a separate Regiment in 1786. In 1862 it became known as the 73rd (Perthshire) Regiment of Foot. In 1881 it re-joined the 42nd Regiment as the 2nd Battalion to form The Black Watch (Royal Highlanders). During its 95 year history the 73rd Regiment served worldwide. While serving in India, it was awarded one of the early Battle Honours for the Siege of Seringapatam in 1799.

The 73rd raised a second battalion in 1808. This battalion later served at Waterloo and The Black Watch is one of the few regiments which can claim to have had two battalions present at the Battle of Waterloo. The second battalion was disbanded in 1817. The 73rd had given up Highland dress in 1809 and its subsequent history is that of a Regiment of the Line (a regiment organised for general service).

The Seringapatam medal, 1799.

The 1st Battalion under the command of Lachlan Macquarie served in Australia from 1810-14. The officers of the 73rd are given the credit for starting the Sydney Races in 1810. Macquarie served as Governor of New South Wales, Australia from 1810 to 1821 and had a leading role in the social, economic and architectural development of the colony. An inscription on his tomb in Scotland describes him as 'The Father of Australia'.

After service in the Kandy Campaign in Ceylon, the 73rd returned to Britain and then took part in the following campaigns:

- The Patriotes Rebellion in Canada in the late 1830s
- The Frontier Wars in South Africa in the 1840s
- The latter part of the Indian Mutiny in the 1850s.

In the mid-1860s they were posted to Hong Kong and spent a number of years in the Far East. One detachment, in fact, was sent to Yokohama in Japan. By 1881 the 73rd had returned to Britain. Under the Cardwell Reforms of 1881 the 42nd and 73rd were reunited.

In 1881 the 73rd Regiment returned home from India and were stationed at Portsmouth. This photograph depicts the 73rd on 23rd February 1881, waiting to be inspected by HSH Prince Edward of Saxe Weimar. Rumour was already rife that the 73rd was soon to become a Highland Regiment again. This may well have been the last occasion which it formally paraded as the 73rd.

South African Campaigns Medal 1834-53.

An officer of the 73rd Regiment, 1786 by A.E. Haswell Miller.

The Birkenhead disaster (1852)

In the early hours of 26th February 1852 Her Majesty's steamer the Birkenhead hit a reef off Danger Point, near Cape Town. It had been carrying 638 troops to South Africa to fight in the Frontier Wars and the 73rd Regiment comprised the largest contingent on board. The hull was penetrated and while many soldiers on the lower decks drowned, order was kept and the women and children were evacuated to the lifeboats. It is thought that the tradition of 'women and children first', known as The Birkenhead Drill, comes from this event.

The wife of a corporal reportedly removed two claret jugs from the sinking ship and hid them beneath her skirts before boarding a lifeboat. They were bought back by the 73rd Regiment after being found in a London sale room a few years later and can now be seen in the Museum. A few survivors made it to the shore and other vessels rescued those who survived at sea. In total 438 drowned, including 56 from the 73rd Regiment. All the women and children were saved. Captain Edward Wright of the 91st Regiment, who was on board the ship, noted that during the ordeal "everyone did as he was directed" and was impressed that all was conducted "with so little noise and confusion". The Duke of Wellington later praised those on board for their conduct.

The Birkenhead claret jugs.

Objects from the Museum collection relating to the Indian Mutiny period (clockwise from top): ornate Indian silver cup; Ghazi shield; dirk with fork, small knife and scabbard; Indian silver filigree box, Indian gold coins; ivory salt and pepper shaker; McVities of Edinburgh oatcake tin, illustrating various scenes of Black Watch valour.

5. The Indian Mutiny, Egypt, the Nile and the South African (or Boer) War (1857-1902)

The Indian Mutiny (1857-59)

In 1857 there was a serious mutiny amongst native troops of the Army in India, in part due to a rumour that cartridges of a newly introduced rifle had been greased with the fat of pigs (deemed unclean by Muslims) or cows (sacred to Hindus). The Mutiny started in Meerut and spread to other garrisons in the North of India. The mutineers captured Delhi and Cawnpore but a small British force managed to hold out in Lucknow. The 42nd arrived in Calcutta in November 1857 and was soon involved in the recapture of Cawnpore, pursuing the retreating mutineers and capturing 15 of their guns. In March 1858 it led the attack on Lucknow where Lieutenant Francis Edward Henry Farquharson was to win the Regiment's first Victoria Cross.

Indian Mutiny Medal, with Bar: Lucknow.

Farquharson's citation reads:

> *For conspicuous bravery, when engaged before Lucknow, on 9 March 1858, in having led a portion of his company, stormed a bastion mounting two guns, and spiked the guns, by which the advanced position held during the night of 9th March was rendered secure from the fire of artillery. Lieutenant Farquharson was severely wounded, while holding an advanced position on the morning of 10th of March.*

The following month, in a much more costly operation, four VCs were awarded for gallantry at the attack on Fort Rooyah and in May 1858 the Regiment had a very fierce fight at Bareilly. In January 1859, just before the Mutiny was finally put down, 37 men of the Regiment were attacked throughout a whole day by over 2,000 mutineers. When the company commander, Captain William Lawson, and all the non-commissioned officers became casualties the post was commanded by private soldiers, two of whom – Walter Cook and Duncan Miller – were awarded the Victoria Cross. This group became known as 'Lawson's Men', now a well-known pipe tune. The 73rd Regiment was also sent to India in 1858 where it arrived in time to take part in the latter stages of suppressing the Mutiny.

Lieutenant Farquharson by Louis William Desanges. Farquharson is depicted winning his Victoria Cross at the Battle of Lucknow in 1858.

The Black Watch

The Black Watch were stationed in India from 1859 to 1867. This photograph from Bareilly shows various forms of dress.

Ram's head snuff mull, possibly used as an ink well before becoming a snuff mull.

The Ashantee War (1873-74)

In 1874 the 42nd was deployed to West Africa in the very brief Ashantee War, which lasted only six weeks. A British Protectorate along the coast of what is now Ghana was being attacked by warriors of the Ashantee tribe. At this time the area was known as the 'white man's grave'. This was a notoriously unhealthy area. The Regiment had to forego wearing Highland dress for the first time. Operating in extremely close bush country against a force of some 15,000 to 20,000 Ashantees, the British brigade could make little advantage of its superior weaponry. In the decisive action at Amoaful, the Regiment led the assault and cleared the enemy from their position. The enemy were then pursued to their capital, Coomassie. After a further action, the town was abandoned by the Ashantees and a peaceful conclusion was then arranged.

Ashantee Medal, with Bar: Coomassie.

The Depot and the Regimental area

In 1873 a permanent Regimental Depot was established in Queens Barracks in Perth, opposite St Ninian's Cathedral. Built in the 1790s, the barracks were named after the first unit to be stationed there: the 4th Queens Own Regiment of Dragoons. The Black Watch has had a long connection with Perthshire and many of the original recruits came from Atholl and the highland part of the county. In 1881, the Cardwell Reforms defined The Black Watch recruiting area as the Counties of Angus, Fife, Perthshire and the City of Dundee.

Soldiers from Queens Barracks pay their respects to their comrades who fell at the battle of the Loos in 1915. The Depot at Queens Barracks was the base for training for the Regiment and the heart of the Regimental Area until the 1960s.

Egypt and the Sudan (1882-85)

The first operations for the 1st Battalion, The Black Watch, were during two consecutive campaigns in Egypt. A rebellion threatened the Suez Canal in which Britain had both a controlling stake and a strategic interest. In a brilliantly conducted operation, The Black Watch was at the front of the Highland Brigade when it stormed the rebel trenches at Tel-el-Kebir in a dawn attack in September 1882. Remaining in Egypt, The Black Watch was next involved in operations against the *Mahdi* – the leader of rebel tribesmen in Egyptian controlled Sudan. In early 1884 it fought in the battles of El Teb and Tamaai. Later that year it took part in the Nile Expedition to relieve General Gordon in Khartoum. After strenuous efforts, advancing with boats up the River Nile, it fought at Kirbekan in February 1885. The expedition was then cancelled on the death of General Gordon.

Egypt Medal, with Bars: Kirbekan, The Nile 1884-85, El-Teb, Suakin 1884 and Tel-el-Kebir.

The Battle of Tel el Kebir.

The Durand Cup

The Durand football competition is the oldest football tournament in India and is still run today. It was started by India's Foreign Secretary, Mortimer Durand, at Simla, India, in 1888. If a team wins the tournament three years for consecutive years they are presented with a cup. The Black Watch won the tournament in 1897, 1898 and 1899. The Durand Cup illustrates the importance of the Scottish diaspora in the spread of football to many parts of the world in the late nineteenth century.

The Durand Cup, donated to the museum in 1971 by the Regiment, is inscribed 'The Durand Football Tournament Challenge Cup, Simla'. It is made of Sterling Silver and was manufactured by Hamilton & Co., Calcutta.

The 1st Battalion with the Durand Cup, 1899.

The South African or Boer War (1899-1902)

The end of the nineteenth century saw the 1st Battalion serving in India and the 2nd Battalion in South Africa fighting in the Boer War. In 1899 the Dutch Boer republics of Transvaal and the Orange Free State invaded the British colonies in Southern Africa. They besieged three towns: Ladysmith, Mafeking and Kimberley. Relief columns were gathered to free them. The 2nd Battalion The Black Watch was with The Highland Brigade in the advance on Kimberley. The Brigade also included: 1st Battalion, Highland Light Infantry; 2nd Battalion, Seaforth Highlanders; and 1st Battalion Argyll & Sutherland Highlanders. 'Black Week' took place in December 1899, when the British Force suffered serious defeats at Stormberg (10th December), Magersfontein (11th December) and Colenso (15th December).

Magersfontein came after several engagements in which the mobility of the Boers enabled them to disengage quickly before their positions were assaulted. Without any proper reconnaissance, the Highland Brigade was ordered to mount a dawn attack. The Black Watch were in the front during this disastrous operation. The Brigade was fired on at close range from a concealed Boer trench, protected by barbed wire. The Battalion suffered heavy casualties, with 93 men killed and 209 wounded. The commander of the Highland Brigade, General Andrew Wauchope, himself a former Commanding Officer of the 2nd Battalion, was one of the first to be killed. As a result of the losses, the 1st Battalion, then serving in India, offered to reinforce the 2nd Battalion. This offer was accepted, and, in December 1901, the 1st Battalion was en route for South Africa. This is one of the few occasions when both regular battalions were on active service together in the same theatre of war. The campaign finally ended with the Treaty of Vereeniging, 31st May 1902.

After the signing of the Treaty, the 2nd Battalion went to India on foreign service and did not return to the United Kingdom until 1919. The principal event was the Coronation Durbar (a ceremonial gathering) for King George V held at Delhi in December 1911. The following year, he became Colonel-in-Chief of the Regiment. The 1st Battalion was stationed at various places in the United Kingdom, the last being Aldershot in 1914 when the Battalion went off to France as part of the British Expeditionary Force

Queens South Africa Medal, with Bars: Paardeberg, Driefontein, Wittebergen, Cape Colony, Transvaal and South Africa 1901; and Kings South Africa Medal, with Bars: South Africa 1901 and 1902.

Uniform of Major General A.G. Wauchope, including: red doublet, officer's sash, white cross belt, officer's sword, dirk and belt.

Sergeants of the 1st and 2nd Battalions, The Black Watch, Hammersmith, 1902. The 1st Battalion was despatched to South Africa in December 1901, to join the 2nd Battalion. By the nature of the two battalion system – with one at home and one abroad – the chances of meeting were remote.

The Black Watch

Lieutenant F.G. "Freddie" Tait

Tait was an amateur golf champion and Black Watch officer. He was well known as a powerful and long hitter of the ball. Tait won the The Amateur Championship twice (1896 and 1898), and finished third in The Open Championship twice (1896 and 1897). Tait was killed in action at Koedoesberg, February 1900. Tait's golf clubs – a putter, a cleek and a mashie – and his pith helmet are on display in the Museum.

The Freddie Tait collection.

Jocks wading barefoot across a river during the Boer War, 1899 to 1902.

Soldiers in the Boer War by W. Skeoch Cumming.

6. Volunteers

During times of national danger, citizens have often formed volunteer units and in the Regimental area many of these have been associated with The Black Watch. Fear of invasion by Napoleon's forces in 1803 led to the raising of the 68th Royal Perthshire Regiment of Militia, which later became the 3rd (Militia) Battalion The Black Watch.

Around 1860 fear of war again caused a spate of volunteer units to be formed. Six of these are of especial interest to the Regiment as they were later to be incorporated into it:

- 1st Forfarshire Rifle Volunteers   (Headquarters: Dundee)
- 2nd Forfarshire Rifle Volunteers   (Headquarters: Friockheim)
- 3rd Forfarshire Rifle Volunteers   (Headquarters: Dundee)
- 1st Perthshire Rifle Volunteers   (Headquarters: Perth)
- 2nd Perthshire Rifle Volunteers   (Headquarters: Birnam)
- 1st Fifeshire Rifle Volunteers   (Headquarters: St Andrews)

Badge of Perthshire Vounteers

Badge of Dundee Vounteers

Badge of Fifeshire Vounteers

*Officer's shako of 1st
Admin Battalion Fifeshire
Rifle Volunteers, 1859-63.*

The Volunteer Battalions were linked to regiments in 1881. With the Haldane Reforms of 1908, the Territorial Force was set up. Thus, there were the 4th (City of Dundee) Battalion, the 5th (Angus & Dundee) Battalion, the 6th (Perthshire) Battalion and the 7th (Fife) Battalion. These Battalions went on to play an important part in both the First and Second World Wars.

In the interwar period and after the Second World War, the volunteers continued in existence as the 4/5th and 6/7th Battalions. In 1967 they were merged to become the 51st Highland Volunteers, the result of yet another re-organisation covering all the volunteer units in the north of Scotland. In 1971 the Volunteers were split into two Battalions. This continued until 1994, when, with the re-naming of volunteer battalions, the 3rd (Volunteer) Battalion The Black Watch was raised. This battalion had a short life. On 1st July 1999, the Battalion was subsumed under the 51st (Highland) Regiment, which again, as in 1967, covers all the volunteer infantry units in the Regimental area. They are now part of 51st Highland, 7th Battalion The Royal Regiment of Scotland. On 28th March 2006, with the formation of the Royal Regiment of Scotland, the unit became the 7th Battalion.

7. The First World War (1914-1918)

The First World War had a devastating effect on the families of Britain. Scotland was no exception. Throughout Angus, Dundee, Fife and Perthshire young men left their homes and went to war. The First World War was the first industrial war the world had experienced. It was later known as 'the war to end all wars' and brought about a loss of life on a scale never seen before. In 1914 many men volunteered in an upsurge of national fervour. Later, as enthusiasm began to wane, persuasive enlistment campaigns and Military Service Acts took the young men of Britain away from their homeland and scattered them around the world to fight for 'King and Country'. The creation of 'Pals Battalions' meant that men from the same village, town or business fought and died alongside each other. The 4th Battalion The Black Watch was almost completely made up of men from Dundee, earning it the nickname 'Dundee's Own'.

The Regiment expanded at an unprecedented rate during the First World War. The recruitment campaign with the message 'Your country needs YOU' caused a flood of over 30,000 men to join. During the First World War over 50,000 men served in the 25 battalions of The Black Watch. They were made up of Regular, Territorial and Service battalions.

- *Regular Battalions generally refers to the 1st and 2nd Battalions, who were in service all the time.*
- *Territorial Battalions were generally made up of part-time volunteer soldiers.*
- *Service Battalions were made up of men recruited into Kitchener's New Army. These included Pals Battalions.*

The 1914-15 Star; British War Medal; and the Allied Victory Medal.

The Battle Honours awarded reflect the famous actions in which the battalions took part. In France and Flanders there were the battles of the Marne, Ypres, Neuve Chappelle, Loos, Arras and the Somme. At the Battle of Loos, six battalions were present. The 4th (City of Dundee) Battalion suffered particularly heavily. As a result it was amalgamated with the 5th (Angus) Battalion. As part of the Meerut Division, the 2nd Battalion was in France and Flanders until late 1915. It fought in Mesopotamia (modern day Iraq). It was present at the Battle of Kut, the Occupation of Baghdad, Istabulat and Tekrit. Later, in Palestine, it was present at the Battle of Megiddo. The 10th Battalion went to Salonika, Greece, in November 1915. It fought at Doiran in Macedonia. The 6th Battalion was awarded the Croix de Guerre by the French Government. This was for the actions at Bois de Courton and Chambrecy in July 1918. When the war came to an end in November 1918 The Black Watch had lost 8,000 men. More than 20,000 had been wounded.

A periscope in use in a trench during the First World War. This avoided exposure to danger from sniper fire while keeping watch.

Trench life during the First World War.

The Black Watch

For freedom and honour

The First World War Memorial Plaque (nicknamed the Dead Man's Penny) and certificate were presented to the next of kin of all those members of His Majesty's Forces who lost their lives in the First World War, either on Active Service or where death was attributable to the War. The period valid for receiving this plaque was 4th August 1914 to 30th April 1920. In August 1917 the government announced a competition in *The Times* newspaper to design the memorial plaque for the families of those lost in the war. The competition was won by Edward Carter Preston. His winning design features the classically robed Britannia, at her feet is a male lion striding forward and to her right is a small dolphin, representing British sea power. Underneath the lion's feet is a smaller lion shown pouncing an eagle. This was meant to represent the hope for the destruction of the Central Powers. Edward Carter Preston's initials are engraved to the right of the lion's forepaw. Above the lion's head is the name of the deceased and 'HE DIED FOR FREEDOM AND HONOUR' is inscribed around the edge. The rank of the deceased was left off the plaque to show the equality of the sacrifice. Over 1,150,000 plaques were issued following the end of the First World War.

Memorial plaque of Thomas Gorrie.

The Wauchope Medallion was specially commissioned by Lieutenant General A.G. Wauchope to commemorate the unrewarded gallantry of 2nd Battalion The Black Watch at various points during the First World War. One example of this was in the capture of Germans trenches on the 25th September 1915. They are treasured as a symbol of the great deeds done by the 2nd Battalion.

Black Watch cap badge with bullet hole.

Samarra railway station, March 1917. It was here that the Bagdad Bell was captured as a trophy. The 2nd Battalion were the first to enter Bagdad when it was taken in March 1917. The Bell remained with the Battalion for the remainder of its existence. It is now housed in the Museum.

The Pipes and Drums playing after the 8th Battalion had captured Longueval on the Somme during the First World War.

After Neuve Chappelle by Shields (from the original by Joseph Gray).

8. The Interwar Period (1919-1939)

During the interwar years, The Black Watch was occupied with garrison duties and international service. At the end of the First World War all front line battalions of The Black Watch were deployed on the Western Front, with the exception of the 2nd Battalion which was in Syria. The demobilisation of the New Army battalions soon followed. In 1922 the Territorial battalions were reduced to two – the 4th and 5th Battalions merged, as did the 6th and 7th Battalions. These battalions were again separated just before the Second World War.

In 1919 the 1st Battalion was posted abroad. It spent 17 years in various garrisons in India and then spent 18 months in the Sudan before returning home to Dover in 1938. Shortly afterwards, hostilities broke out, marking the beginning of the Second World War. The 2nd Battalion spent two years in Germany. It formed part of the international force overseeing the referendum in Upper Silesia. Thereafter it was on home postings for 15 years. The 2nd Battalion was deployed on active service to Palestine in 1937: combating Arab gangs; patrolling; carrying out searches and ambushes; and providing village garrisons.

General Service Medal, Palestine.

Objects from the Museum collection relating to actions in France and Germany during the Second World War (clockwise from top): illustrated map tray, depicting actions from the Second World War; water bottle; pocket watch; cigarette case with bullet hole of R.P. Mossman; Highland Division medallion; sun compass used in North Africa; pocket watch of Sid Lunn.

9. The Second World War (1939-1945)

During the Second World War, there were, at various points, some 13 Battalions of the Regiment, of which seven were front line battalions serving in a number of Theatres of War. The Black Watch lost nearly 1,400 officers and men during the War.

The 1st, 5th and 7th Battalions in the 51st Highland Division

All the kilted Highland regiments were represented in the 51st Highland Division. It served with great distinction throughout its history. Its exploits in the Second Word War earned it a legendary status. The Division was deployed to France in January 1940. By the time of the German attack in May 1940, it included both the 1st and 4th Battalions. The Division fought a rear-guard action back to St Valery-en-Caux. On 12th June, having run out of ammunition and food, General Victor Fortune, the commander of the 51st Highland Division, was forced to surrender to General Erwin Rommel. The 1st Battalion were taken as prisoners of war. Fortunately, the 4th Battalion was evacuated through Le Havre.

Standard issue helmet, recovered from the sea at St Valery-en-Caux more than 50 years after the surrender.

The 51st Highland Division was then reconstituted and included three Black Watch battalions: a re-formed 1st Battalion, the 5th Battalion, and the 7th Battalion. During 1942 the Division served in Egypt and took part in the victory at El Alamein on 23rd October 1942. It was then at the forefront of the pursuit of the German and Italian forces across the Libyan Desert with the Black Watch battalions being engaged in all the major actions.

After North Africa, the Division spearheaded the invasion of Sicily and it landed on 10th July 1943. Tough resistance was met later in the month-long fight for Sicily. The Division then withdrew from the Mediterranean Theatre to prepare for the invasion of Normandy. The 5th Battalion landed in Normandy on D Day (6th June 1944). It was soon involved in bitter fighting at Breville and Colombelles. All three battalions were committed to the breakout from the Normandy Bridgehead during August. Thereafter, little opposition was encountered until Holland. Here, the Division took part in various operations.

It played a part in stemming the German counter-offensive in the Ardennes in January 1945. This was followed by the Battle of the Reichswald Forest during February 1945. This included some of the bitterest fighting of the whole war. On 23rd March the Division crossed the Rhine and the 7th Battalion was the first British battalion to cross. The war in Europe ended in May 1945.

The commander of the 51st Highland Division, Major General Tom Gordon Rennie, was a regular Black Watch officer, an escapee from St Valery, and a former Commanding Officer of the 5th Battalion in 1942. He was killed at the Rhine Crossing, 24th March 1945.

The 2nd Battalion

The 2nd Battalion had a remarkably varied war, fighting across the globe, from Africa, to the Mediterranean, to South East Asia. On the outbreak of hostilities it was already on active service in Palestine. By August 1940 it was facing vastly superior Italian Forces in British Somaliland. When French resistance collapsed the situation became unstable and British Forces were evacuated. But not before the Battalion fought a successful day-long rearguard action at Barkasan where it had to resort to a number of bayonet charges.

In May 1941, the 2nd Battalion was deployed in the defence of the Greek island of Crete. It was subjected to a German parachute assault preceded by heavy bombing. The initial drops were made onto the Battalion positions around Heraklion airfield. This was at great cost to the Germans with few Black Watch casualties. On subsequent days, drops were made outside the defended perimeter and a large German force built up. Royal Naval ships entered Heraklion harbour by night and evacuated the garrison without alerting the enemy. But from dawn onwards the shipping was subjected to hours of continuous air attack resulting in casualties on the voyage to Egypt.

By early July 1941 the Battalion was deployed to Syria for action against Vichy French forces. After an armistice was signed, in October 1941 it moved to the besieged garrison of Tobruk on the Libyan coast. On 21st November it was tasked with a major role in the attempted breakout from Tobruk. This was timed to coincide with the advance of the 8th Army from the east. Although the Battalion captured its objectives it did so without the planned armoured support. This resulted in terrible loss in the face of concentrated German machine gun, rifle and artillery fire. Of the 32 officers and 600 men who started the attack, two hours later only eight officers and 160 men remained uninjured. The commander of the Battalion at this time was Colonel George Rusk, one of the founders of the Museum.

In early 1942 the 2nd Battalion was moved to India as part of the reinforcements to oppose the Japanese invasion of India. It remained there until March 1944 and took part in activity against local unrest, a rescue operation after a severe cyclone at Contai, and a short spell in the line at Arakan. After completing six months training, the Battalion was flown into the jungles of Burma as part of General Wingate's Long Range Penetration Group, or Chindits.

There, operating behind Japanese lines it fought for five months in the most appalling conditions of heat, monsoon and disease. It carried out ambushes and sabotage against the enemy. In one operation some 200 men of the Battalion ambushed and broke up a column of 1,200 Japanese.

In September 1944 the Battalion returned to India. After being nursed back to health, it was trained as a parachute unit. Before it could be deployed for the invasion of Malaya against Japan, the war had come to an end.

The 4th and 6th Battalions

The 4th and 6th Battalions also served in France in 1940, but escaped at Dunkirk. Their later histories are somewhat different. The 4th spent the greater part of the War on garrison duties in Gibraltar before returning to the United Kingdom in November 1943. The 6th served in North Africa, the Italian mainland (Cassino) and Greece.

The Tyneside Scottish

The 1st Tyneside Scottish became a Territorial Battalion of The Black Watch in 1939 and served in France, 1940 (Ficheux), Iceland, and North West Europe (Defence of Rauray). The Battalion was disbanded in October 1944 and the men sent to other units (including Black Watch battalions).

Field Marshall The Earl Archibald Percival Wavell (1883-1950)

Wavell is the most famous son of The Black Watch and known to thousands of soldiers in the British Empire during the Second World War. As Commander-in-Chief Middle East he fought with great skill against the Axis Forces in the Western Desert and Ethiopia. He was overwhelmingly successful in these operations and the German General Erwin Rommel, considered him to be "the only British general with a touch of genius". Later, as Supreme Commander South West Pacific in the war against the Japanese he was recognised as an outstanding administrator, and as Viceroy and Governor General of India, he negotiated part of the difficult process which ultimately led to independence for the Indian sub-continent. Wavell was Colonel of The Regiment from 1946 to 1950.

Field Marshall Wavell by Simon Elwes.

The 1939-45 Star; North Africa Star, with Bar: 8th Army; Italy Star; France and Germany Star; Defence Medal; War Medal; and Burma Star.

Pipe Major Rab Roy, playing for injured troops in the Regimental Aid Post after the 2nd Battalion breakout from Tobruk. Roy became known as the Piper of Tobruk.

A 6-pounder anti-tank detachment relaxes near Monte Cassino, May 1944.

Men of the 2nd Battalion, carrying out arduous preparatory training, in advance of deployment to face the Japanese advance through Burma, late 1943.

Men from the 7th (Fife Territorial) Battalion marching across the arid North Afarican desert. In June 1942, the re-formed 51st Highland Division arrived in Egypt to play a major role in the Battle of El Alamein.

Privates Bruce and McMichael, Sfax, 10th April 1943. Often referred to as the "Highway Decorators", members of the 51st Highland Division were immensely proud of their reputation and of their Divisional sign.

Victory Parade in the ruined streets of Bremerhaven 15th May 1945.

Objects from the Museum collection relating to the Korean campaign (clockwise from top left): Corporal's badge of rank; mug, issued Christmas 1952, in which tea and rum was served to the Other Ranks by Officers; Chinese spade; Chinese horn; Chinese pipe; Chinese, Communist and United Nations propaganda; South Korean flag; Chinese lighter.

10. 1945 - 1955

On 26 February 1948 The Black Watch was the last British battalion to leave the newly independent Pakistan. When they marched out of Napier Barracks to board the troopship *Empire Halladale* they were thanked by President Mohammed Ali Jinnah. This brought to an end a 150 year connection with the Indian sub-continent. From 1945 until 1952 the 1st Battalion served in various parts of Germany until it returned to Crail, having been warned of forthcoming service in Korea. A detachment of volunteers had already gone to the Argyll and Sutherland Highlanders and on the return of that Regiment had transferred to the King's Own Scottish Borderers. On 13th May 1952, the Colonel-in-Chief, Queen Elizabeth, The Queen Mother, visited the 1st Battalion at Crail to bid the Battalion farewell. This was her first major engagement since the death of her husband, HM King George VI.

Korea (1952-53)

In June 1950 the Communist North Koreans invaded South Korea. After initial success, the North Koreans were held back by a United Nations force, sent to assist the South Korean government. Chinese troops then entered the conflict in support of the fellow communist North Koreans. The 1st Battalion was deployed to Korea in June 1952 as part of the 1st Commonwealth Division on HM Troopship *Empire Orwell,* which berthed in Pusan harbour on 20th June 1952. It was soon in the line, under the command of Lieutenant Colonel David Rose, and took over from the 1st Battalion the Royal Australian Regiment on 8th July. During its time in Korea, the Battalion fought an entirely defensive war. It held hill-top positions and faced Chinese troops where two notable battles were both fought on a position known as The Hook, in November 1952 and May 1953. The Black Watch lost some 66 men in Korea. The majority are buried at the United Nations War Cemetery in Pusan.

The Korean War Medal and United Nations Korea Medal.

A memorial service was held in Pusan on Sunday 12th July 1953, the day before The Black Watch left Korea. It commemorated the officers and men of the Battalion who had died during the conflict Pictured are Reverend Tom Nicol and Lieutenant Colonel David Rose.

Pipe Major Erickson (left) and Lance Corporal McNie play for Chief of Staff US Army, General Collins, and Commanding Officer, Lieutenant Colonel David Rose.

The Black Watch

Kenya (1953-55)

Immediately after action in the Korean War, on their return home, the Battalion was deployed to Kenya in 1953 to help suppress the Mau-Mau Rebellion. Kenya, with much of Africa, had been colonised by the British in the nineteenth century. European settlers had been carving out farms in the rich hill country of the Kenyan plateau. The Mau Mau uprising of 1952 to 1960 was an insurgency by Kenyan tribesmen against British colonial rule. The resistance was formed by members of the Kikuyu ethnic group. The Kikuyu called their freedom fighters Mau Mau. The British Government called them rebels. The Uprising hastened Kenyan independence. It motivated Africans in other countries to fight against colonial rule. Kenya became independent in 1963. The 1st Battalion returned to Glasgow on 27th April 1955.

*Africa General Service medal,
with Bar: Kenya.*

On Christmas Eve 1953, Major The Earl A.J.A. Wavell (son of A.P. Wavell) was killed in action in Kenya. He was one of six men who died in Kenya during the operations.

2nd Battalion

The 2nd Battalion was amalgamated with the 1st Battalion in July 1948. It was reformed in April 1952 and served in British Guyana, 1954-56. It was finally disbanded in October 1956.

*Objects from the Museum
collection relating to the Kenyan
campaign (clockwise from top
left): mug and case of Major
The Earl A.J.A. Wavell; Mau
Mau weapons including: spear,
quiver, home-made rifle, panga
and arrows; animal skin.*

The Black Watch

11. 1956 – 2006

Between 1956 and 2006 the 1st Battalion served in Germany (as part of the British Army of the Rhine), Cyprus, Gibraltar, Northern Ireland, Hong Kong, and Belize, as well as various postings within the United Kingdom.

Queens Barracks, Perth

In 1961, the Regimental Depot at Queens Barracks, Perth, was closed. Recruits trained at the Barracks had seen action in the Sudan, South Africa, both World Wars, Korea and Kenya. With the end of National Service and the much smaller intake of recruits, it was decided that their training should be done on a more centralised basis. Initially, it was planned that this should take place at Bridge of Don, near Aberdeen. Later it was to be further centralised on a Scottish Division basis at Glencorse, near Edinburgh. In 1962 the Regimental Headquarters and Museum moved to Balhousie Castle, Perth. The final recruit squad passed out of Queens Barracks on 11th March 1961.

The final parade at Queens Barracks, Perth, in 1961.

Cyprus

The United Nations Peacekeeping Force in Cyprus (UNFICYP) was established in 1964. It was to prevent a recurrence of fighting between the Greek Cypriots and Turkish Cypriots, to contribute to the maintenance and restoration of law and order, and a return to normal conditions. The Black Watch served with the United Nations Peacekeeping Force in Cyprus in 1966-67.

General Service Medal,
Cyprus.

UN Cyprus medal.

*Private McCarthy leads the donkey train, followed by
Privates Steadman and Quin, Cyprus.*

*Archbishop Makarios, the newly elected President of the Republic of Cyprus, during his first official visit the Sovereign
Base Area of Episkopi in late 1960. The Guard of Honour was formed by A Company.*

The Black Watch

Northern Ireland

In August 1969, British soldiers were deployed on the streets of Northern Ireland. Their role was to help restore law and order after widespread rioting and public disorder. What started as a civil rights campaign soon became an armed struggle by republicans. Operation BANNER was a military deployment in aid of the Civil Power in Northern Ireland. It was the longest continuous campaign undertaken by the British Army. At the height of the Troubles, over 25,000 troops were deployed to the Province. During the 38 years of the campaign, 697 servicemen were killed. The 1st Battalion completed 11 operational tours in Northern Ireland. They varied in length from a few weeks to two years.

Lance Corporal Hay and Privates Cowie and Percival practice debussing, Armagh, Northern Ireland.

General Service Medal, Northern Ireland.

A road block by men of A Company, while stationed at Ballykinler, Co. Down in 1976, during their first tour of that station.

Hong Kong

In June 1997 the Colony of Hong Kong was handed over to the People's Republic of China. It was the last significant part of the British Empire. The 1st Battalion played a prominent role in the ceremony, which was concluded in a torrential downpour.

Farewell Parade, 30th of June 1997

Kosovo

Following the breakup of the former Yugoslavia, violence broke out between the various communities. The North Atlantic Treaty Organisation (NATO) deployed a multinational force to establish a safe and secure environment for the people of Kosovo.

The 1st Battalion were deployed as the main British contingent of Headquarters Kosovo Force between July and November 2001.

Iraq

Early in 2003, the 1st Battalion was deployed to Iraq, as part of the British Forces on Operation Telic. It spent the months from February until June in the southern area of the country around Basrah. After the tour of duty the Battalion returned to Fallingbostel and in 2004 was posted to Warminster in Wiltshire as Demonstration Battalion. It was deployed to Iraq for a second time in late summer 2004. The Battalion was once more based around Basrah. Later, however, the Battalion was moved up-country to Camp Dogwood, to assist the United States Forces in Operation Bracken. The Battalion returned to Warminster in December 2004. The Regiment lost a total of seven men during the two tours in Iraq.

In November 2005, the 1st Battalion was awarded two Battle Honours: Iraq 2003; and Al Basrah. These were the last battle honours awarded to The Black Watch as a Regiment.

British Army vest with Kevlar protective plate, including bullet holes, dated to 2003.

Amalgamation

On 28th March 2006 a new multi-battalion Scottish regiment was formed. After 276 years as an independent regiment, the 1st Battalion, The Black Watch (Royal Highland Regiment) became The Black Watch, 3rd Battalion, The Royal Regiment of Scotland.

The Black Watch Collect

O God, whose strength setteth fast the mountains,

Lord of the hills to whom we lift our eyes;

Grant us grace that we, of The Black Watch,

Once chosen to watch the mountains of an earthly Kingdom,

May stand fast in the faith and be strong,

Until we come to the heavenly Kingdom of Him,

Who has bidden us watch and pray,

Thy Son, Our Saviour and Lord.

Amen.

Objects from the Museum collection relating to campaigns in Cyprus, Hong Kong and Northern Ireland (clockwise from top left): caltrop used in Northern Ireland; arm band and cap, with United Nations insignia, worn in Cyprus; rubber bullets used in Northern Ireland; Colonial flag flown in Hong Kong before independence in 1997.

12. The Black Watch, 3rd Battalion, The Royal Regiment of Scotland

Since the formation of the Royal Regiment of Scotland, The Black Watch Battalion has carried out the following operations tours.

Iraq

In October 2006, Alpha (Grenadier) Company deployed to Iraq on a seven month tour. They formed part of 19 Light Brigade under the operational control of the Danish Battlegroup, operating in the rural north of Basrah Province.

In 2007 13 Platoon, D Company deployed to Iraq and was attached to 2nd Battalion, The Royal Welsh. Two men of the Platoon were killed by an Improvised Explosive Device.

Afghanistan (2009)

In April 2009 The Black Watch was deployed to the Helmand Province of Afghanistan. This was 61 years after the 2nd Battalion left Pakistan and the North West Frontier. The Battalion was part of the International Security Assistance Force operating in support of the Afghan Government and Afghan National Army. The Black Watch formed the Regimental Battle Group South (RBG(S)). The RBG(S) consisted of two rifle companies, a fire support company group and combat support attachments. The Black Watch was operating directly to the Divisional Commander in the South as his only manoeuvre force element (operating outside static bases) in the six provinces of southern Afghanistan. The task was extremely demanding and relied in the use of helicopter assets. Delta Company was attached to the 2nd Battalion, The Mercian Regiment, to form an Operational Mentoring and Liaison Team. It worked with in Helmand Province, training and mentoring the Afghan National Army. Twelve members of the Battalion also served with the Elite Brigade Reconnaissance Force. The battalion lost five men during this deployment.

Operational Service Medal, with Bar: Afghanistan

Corporal Rab Lindsay pipes as the Battalion saltire is raised in Camp Roberts.

On operations in Afghanistan.

13. Royal Colonels

Colonels-in-Chief were Royal patrons. The Black Watch has had only three during its history.

King George V	1912 - 1936
Her Majesty Queen Elizabeth The Queen Mother	1937-2002
His Royal Highness The Prince Charles, Duke of Rothesay	2003-2006

In 2006 The Black Watch became the 3rd Battalion, The Royal Regiment of Scotland. The Colonel-in-Chief of the Royal Regiment of Scotland is Her Majesty Queen Elizabeth. The Duke of Rothesay remains the Royal Colonel of The Black Watch.

Her Majesty Queen Elizabeth The Queen Mother by Von Marientrier.

Colonel-in-Chief uniform of George V.

Duke of Rothesay by Georgina Barclay.

The Black Watch

14. Balhousie Castle

The origins of Balhousie Castle are said to date back to the twelfth century. Originally an L-shaped tower house, what we see today is the central part, possibly dating from the seventeenth century. In its present form, the Castle dates from the 1860s. Documents with reference to Balhousie Castle date back to the fifteenth century. In 1422, Murdoch, Duke of Albany granted the Barony of Balhousie to John Eviot. The property remained in the Eviot family until 1609. There was a brief interlude in which the Mercers, a well-known family in the Burgh of Perth, had possession of the property. In 1609 the lands were sold by Colin Eviot to John Mathew, son of Robert Mathew, merchant of Perth. The property then passed to Andrew Grant and John Lamb.

On 27th September 1625, King Charles I granted to Master Francis Hay, his heirs and assignees, the lands and barony of Balhousie. He was the son of Peter Hay of Rattray and was a writer to the Signet before 1617. He acquired several properties in Perthshire and Wigtownshire, including the barony of Dupplin in 1642. He was fined £2,000 sterling under Cromwell's Act of Grace and Pardon in 1654. He was succeeded by his son George (died 1672), who in turn was succeeded by his son Thomas. Thomas Hay of Balhousie was the Member of Parliament for Perthshire in the 1690s. He was created Viscount Dupplin, with remainder to heirs-male of his body on 31st December 1697. William, sixth Earl of Kinnoull, died unmarried in London on 10th May 1709 and Thomas succeeded to the title as seventh Earl. He was suspected of favouring the Jacobites and was imprisoned in Edinburgh Castle, dying four years later.

The succession of Earls continued:

- George Henry, eighth Earl, Member of Parliament for Fowey (Cornwall)

- Thomas, ninth Earl, Member of Parliament for Cambridge

- Robert Auriol Hay Drummond, who succeeded his uncle as tenth Earl. He was appointed Lord Lyon King of Arms, which was then a sinecure.

- His son, Thomas Robert, succeeded as eleventh Earl. He was Colonel of the Royal

- Perthshire Militia, 1809-55, Lord Lieutenant of the County and succeeded his father as Lord Lyon, King of Arms. It was he who extended the Castle.

The Hays did not live at Balhousie Castle: their main residence was at Dupplin. By the early 1860s the castle was in a dilapidated state. Only the first floor was inhabited. Thomas Robert restored the Castle and added two wings to the original L-shaped tower house.

The architect he employed was David Smart. The building was then let out. The tenants included, Henry Hay Norie, a lawyer, John Shields of Wallace Works, who died in 1889 and James Ramsay, a jute broker. The Hay family came to live at the Castle around 1912 and remained until 1926. The Castle then became a convent. The nuns were from the Society of St Peter and were associated with St Ninian's Episcopal Cathedral. They appear to have resided in the castle until about 1940. During the Second World War, the property was used by the Auxiliary Training Service as Officers' Quarters. After the War, it housed a detachment of the Royal Army Service Corps and the Headquarters, Highland District, Corps of Royal Engineers. In the early 1960s there was a major Army re-organisation: The Black Watch Depot at Queens Barracks was closed and Regimental Headquarters and The Black Watch Museum came to the castle where they remain to this day.

The historic Colours of the 6th Battalion were laid up in the Regimental Museum, Balhousie Castle, 1986.

Balhousie Castle today.

A short history of the Regiment

Further Reading

Fergusson, Bernard, *The Black Watch and the King's Enemies, London*: Collins 1950.

Fergusson, Bernard, *The Black Watch, A Short History*, Perth: Woods, 2002.

Linklater, Eric and Andro, *The Black Watch*, London: Barrie & Jenkins, 1977.

Lindsay, S.J. (ed), *The Black Watch Photographic Archive*, Stroud: Tempus, 2000.

Parker, John, *The Black Watch, The Inside Story of the Oldest Highland Regiment in the British Army*, London: Headline, 2005.

Royle, Trevor, *The Black Watch, A Concise History*, Edinburgh: Mainstream, 2006.

Samson, J.L.R., *A Concise Account to The Black Watch and Its Movements*, Perth: Woods, 2001.

Wauchope, A.G., *A History of The Black Watch in the Great War*, London: The Medici Society, 1925-26.

The Red Hackle, the Regimental magazine, 1921 to date.

Acknowledgments

This publication was written, collated and edited by Emma Halford-Forbes and Tommy Smyth, The Black Watch Caste & Museum, and edited by David Strachan, Perth & Kinross Heritage Trust.

The basis of much of this publication has come from other Archive and Museum publications, interpretation and exhibitions. With thanks to those who helped draft and proof the text for this publication: Major (Retd) RJW Proctor, Lieutenant Colonel (Retd) RM Riddell, Lieutenant Colonel (Retd) Stephen Lindsay, Ruari Halford-MacLeod, Jill van Millingen, Richard McKenzie, and a raft of Museum staff and volunteers.

With thanks to John McKenzie and Frank Proctor, who took many of the images in this publication.